Winged
Victory:

Altered Images

....

૭

Winged Victory:
Altered Images

Transcending Breast Cancer

୭

Revised and Expanded

Photographs by Art Myers

Foreword by David Spiegel, MD
Author of *Living Beyond Limits*

Introduction by Dani Grady
Director of Outreach and Communications, San Diego Cancer Center
Co-Founder of Cancer Survivorship: San Diego!

Introduction by Annick Parent
Co-Founder of *les amazones s'exposent*
Author of *Itinéraire d'une amazone*

Original Poetry by Maria Marrocchino

Photographic Gallery of Fine Art Books, San Diego, California

Winged Victory: Altered Images
Transcending Breast Cancer

....

ISBN 978-1-889169-01-9

Library of Congress Control Number 2009934245

Editor: Diane Rush

Original photographs are available for exhibition and/or purchase.

For information, contact:
Photographic Gallery of Fine Art Books
P.O. Box 370175
San Diego, CA 92137
Fax 619-223-5744
art@artmyers.com

This book is dedicated to my wife Stephanie Myers who is always enthusiastically supportive of my good endeavors and benignly tolerant of my quixotic adventures.

And to Annick Parent, my "French Connection" who introduced me to the French breast cancer support community and in the process became a dear friend.

ço

Acknowledgements

It is no small task to put together a book such as this. It couldn't have been accomplished without the help of important friends.

My first recognition must go to the women who were brave enough to reveal themselves in these photographs and to tell a bit about their journey through the breast cancer experience. Brava to each of you. You are pioneers.

I give a special thank-you to two women who gave invaluable aid: Dani Grady who helped conceptualize the project and has lent support in many ways, and Annick Parent who drew me into the breast cancer support community in France. Both of these women are themselves photographic subjects in the book and each has written an introduction.

I thank the documentary filmmaker Anja Unger, her producer Bernard Bloch and her film crew Pascale Mons, Arlette Girarot and Stefanie Rieke for all their support, as well as for their help in recruiting photographic subjects in France. Further, I won't soon forget their assistance in lugging my photo equipment up to those 5th and 6th floor Paris walk-up apartments.

Importantly, I also thank Maria Marrocchino for the beautiful poetry, as well as Lillian Stirling and Natacha Tullier for their assistance with the translation.

And lastly, a very special hug of appreciation to my editor Diane Rush. Free with suggestions and not afraid to voice needed criticism, she was the tireless anchor of this project.

About *Winged Victory: Altered Images Transcending Breast Cancer*

"A very moving and important work."

-Feminist Bookstore News

"Real stories...real people."

-Glamour Magazine

"The powerful effect of this book is exhilarating. This book is necessary and encouraging for cancer survivors, their loved ones and others who challenge themselves in life."

-Small Press Magazine

"An inspiring portrayal of courage, confidence and joy inviting the reader to 'see this radiant body...on this perfect woman.' This is a book to share and it should be prominently displayed in all health care facilities that deal with breast cancer."

-Steve Brock,
Book Reviews on the Internet

"A tremendously important work."

-Kevin McCormick, KRON-TV,
San Francisco

"Wow, what a fabulous book. I couldn't put it down...I was so inspired and uplifted to see all of these beautiful women share their breast cancer experiences."

-Sara, San Diego, Breast Cancer Survivor

Also by Art Myers

....

Women First

A photographic series documenting women who are HIV positive

Nyumbani

A photographic monograph of children with HIV/AIDS living in an orphanage in Africa

The Song of Nyumbani

A dance film featuring images from *Nyumbani*

Contact the Author

....

Art Myers
Photographic Gallery of Fine Art Books
P.O. Box 370175
San Diego, CA 92137
Fax 619-223-5744
art@artmyers.com

Winged Victory of Samothrace
The Louvre, Paris

Foreword

There is great beauty in a woman's form. Yet what is it that is so endlessly fascinating about it? It is not simply the curves, the pleasingly familiar yet forever varied arrangement of breasts, stomach, thighs. It is the spirit which moves her, makes her part of something more. Thus the Winged Victory of Samothrace stirs one not as a piece of stone with arms amputated and wings attached. As one approaches it from below and climbs the staircase to it in the Louvre, one's breath is taken away by its power: female strength transcending the ravages of time.

The images in this book are of female strength. There is no pretense here, no gaze averted. One woman diagnosed with breast cancer in 1942 was told never to show her scar to her husband. Bad advice. She flourished in the ensuing half century with a husband who was quite willing to see and touch all of her body.

Breast cancer is not a good thing, and the loss of a breast is something nobody wants. Yet when it happens, the women in this book are telling us, you are forced to reassess the beauty in your life and in your body. Hiding the loss, the scar, implies shame. It then is not merely the breast that is gone, but yourself as a woman, as a source of beauty, as someone deserving tenderness and the admiration of a lover.

The women in these photos did something different. On these pages they say, "Here I am." They are redefining their beauty: breasts missing, reconstructed, they present their bodies and themselves with humor, sadness, vulnerability, honesty. They challenge us to look beyond what is missing, beneath the scar. They evoke admiration: of their beauty and their courage. They do not hide their loss, they transcend it.

I have listened to groups of women with breast cancer for some two decades. None are happy about the disease or its effects on their bodies. But they yearn to be treated as people, not cases, to be seen as the women they are, not as "damaged goods." They learn not to retreat from cancer but to live with it: "I realized one day that in order to fully accept who I was, I had to learn to love my cancer. It is a part of me, like it or not. To love myself I had to learn to love it." They learn to focus on what they are, rather than what they are not.

The paradox is that in order to be appreciated for who you are, you have to admit being something others may fear or dislike: "tainted by cancer." By saying openly, "I have cancer," you can get on to "now what?" I am this, but I am also more than this. I am a woman, a lover, a friend, a wife. These women say to other women with cancer, "Don't hide your cancer from yourself or anyone else. Admit it and live beyond it." They also call on us to re-examine what constitutes beauty, both physical and mental. These women and their men are beautiful and interesting, each in their personal way. They make the viewer comfortable because they are comfortable. They show us that they can live with and beyond their cancer, the damage to their bodies, the threat to their lives. It is not easy, but it can be done. They show us how. Enjoy them. They remind us of what is vital and beautiful in life.

by David Spiegel, MD
Professor of Psychiatry and Behavioral Sciences
Stanford University School of Medicine
Author of *Living Beyond Limits:
New Hope and Help for Facing Life-Threatening Illness.*
Ballantine Books, 1994

Preface

I am still haunted by the memory of the phone call from my mother telling me in a trembling voice that my sister, Joanne, still in her thirties, had been diagnosed with breast cancer. Following a prolonged, heroic battle to survive, she was to eventually die from that disease. Two decades later, I anxiously faced a surgeon in an antiseptic hospital waiting room as he uttered the dreaded words, "Your wife has breast cancer."

In my career as a physician I have many times had the sobering responsibility of delivering the news of a cancer diagnosis to patients and their loved ones. However, I was not prepared for the overwhelming effect that breast cancer in two close family members would have on my life. I began to see the disease in a new light. I learned that anxiety about survival, initially the most important worry, can give way later to a new unease both in the survivor and her partner. The woman may begin to cover her nakedness, fearing a spouse's averted glance, or turn away from the reflection in a mirror that unremittingly reminds her of fears of diminished femininity. A partner withdraws a hand to avoid touching a scar which once was a graceful curve. Lovers draw apart, an absent breast now a barrier to their intimacy. A fiancé quietly turns his back and walks out of a cancer survivor's life. These fears about body image, femininity, and sexuality are understandable in a society that is bombarded by media messages of centerfolds, push-up bras and silicone implants—messages that erroneously imply that a perfect breast is the requisite icon of the feminine essence.

With the support of my wife Stephanie, now a two-decade survivor and one of the women in the book, I undertook this photographic project hoping to show that a woman's fundamental nature is not dependent on anything external; the loss of part or all of her breast is not a threat to her being. The short narratives, written by the women and their partners, are included as an important part of the message. With no substantive editing they come right from the subjects' hearts, printed as written. The beautiful poems were created especially for this book.

In my other career, that of fine art photographer, I had already been photographing women for 15 years. But it wasn't until I started this project that I began to understand the many elements that make a woman's image complete. Now it is my hope that these pictures, poems and personal vignettes will reveal the persistence of a woman's beauty, strength and femaleness in all of its complexity, even after the transforming experience of breast cancer.

Art Myers

Preface to Second Edition

On first thought I planned not to publish a second edition of this book. It is very time demanding and intensive work putting together a volume such as this. But as the first edition coasted to the end of its long run and the last book was sent to the distributor, the confluence of two events caused me to change my mind.

One mellow Saturday afternoon I was searching for something in a storage cabinet and ran across a stack of guest books from the many exhibitions of the book's photographs. Over the years the book's images and vignettes have appeared in numerous galleries and museums across the USA as well as in several foreign countries. In a reflective mood I squatted on the floor in the middle of the room and began to scan the numerous comments scribed into the books by exhibition visitors.

Oft repeated words about the images began to leap out at me from the dozens of pages I thumbed through:

"Helped me through my own breast cancer experience."
"Moving."
"Needs to be seen by everyone."
"Should be in every cancer treatment facility."
"Empowers me."
"A profound statement about breast cancer."
"Powerful message."

I was touched by the poignancy and honesty of these messages.

Shortly thereafter I received a letter from Annick, a French woman you will meet in this book. Herself a breast cancer survivor, she told of how the images from the book inspired her through her own treatment ordeal and asked me if

I would allow my photographs to be shown in an exhibition in France. A friendship developed between us and through this relationship the way was eventually opened for me to photograph several breast cancer survivors in France. I discovered that these women live with the same hopes and dreams and fears and stigmas as do those in the USA. With these new images in hand it became apparent that a second edition of *Winged Victory* should be published.

We have honored these French women's requests that their narratives be printed in both English and French.

– AM

Table of Contents

Introduction

When I was diagnosed with breast cancer as a young woman of 29, it was easy to despair at the perceived loss of my figure and dating future. I had never seen a woman depicted in our pop culture as a "mastectomy beauty." The gift of a lifetime came to me from the sisterhood of strangers who reached out to share their metamorphic journey from breast cancer victim to woman of substance.

As executive director of the University of California San Diego Cancer Center's Thrivers' Network, a cancer patients' support program, I met many breast cancer survivors who are truly phenomenal women. They exude beauty, strength and confident femininity. For years I envisioned a photo essay reflecting this spirit. In my original concept the photos would capture the women in elegant poses with leis and necklaces averting the eye from imperfections while retaining the classic notion of beauty.

Then I met Art Myers.

He thought it was vital that the women openly expose their scars. This revelatory act would also make acceptance a visible and essential concomitant of beauty. Art was passionate on this point. He had been dreaming of this project since his wife Stephanie's treatment for breast cancer.

He was right. We have all known that when a woman facing breast cancer asks her doctor to show her a picture of a woman who has had breast surgery, she is shown a photo from a textbook of a scarred disembodied torso in harsh clinic light. In this impersonal context, the loss of body parts and marks of the knife are "disfigurement."

This alienation from ourselves was a common

experience for many of the women in this project. One by one we came to see our involvement as a way to change perception. This became our rallying point. We gained unity and strength in our determination to set the record straight. When I approached Dora, an eighty-three-year-old church-going great-grandmother and fifty-year survivor she immediately said, "I will, I absolutely will! Nothing has changed in the past fifty years!"

The women in these photos have revealed the most private aspects of their lives. They have done so as a gift of mentoring and in hope for change.

The models come from varied backgrounds. They are a lawyer, nurse, secretary, professor, executive, activist, clerk, administrator, radiology technician, psychologist, schoolteacher and homemaker. No one had posed nude before or even had the desire to do so. There was a common feeling of modesty, some being more shy than others. Most were skeptical of their ability to convey their sense of beauty to the camera. However, no one has regretted her participation and all are very proud of their photos.

With the progression of this project I witnessed in these women an enhanced sense of self-esteem and pride in their bodies. There is now no secrecy shadowing the metamorphosis of their self-image. Revealed are women of substance, the sisterhood.

by Dani Grady
Director of Outreach and Communications, San Diego Cancer Center
Co-Founder of Cancer Survivorship: San Diego!

Introduction

When the doctors told me that I was going to lose a breast, I wanted to know what I would look like asymmetrical. "Can you show me some photographs of women living with one breast?" I asked. In reply they had not a single image, not a single description. Searching elsewhere in books and magazines proved just as unhelpful. So discovering Art Myers' photographs displayed in this book was a revelation for me. The powerful images showed me that there was somewhere beyond cancer; somewhere beyond mastectomy.

In France there is a stigma to living with a missing breast. Although the majority of women undergoing mastectomy in France elect not to have reconstruction, media articles on living after breast cancer focus mostly on women who have had reconstruction. They tend to ignore, or seem to mention only

in passing, those choosing to live with a missing breast (or two). In Myers' photos I discovered women with whom I could identify—Andrea, Dani, Susan, and others—all asymmetric like me.

Everything changed for me the day I discovered those photographs. I could now imagine myself living with a single breast without provoking an attack of anxiety. I immediately wanted other women who had gone through, or will go through, the breast cancer experience to benefit from this message of life and freedom told by our American sisters through the images and personal vignettes in this book. Subsequently, Lillian Stirling and I created the French association *les amazones s'exposent*. Named after the mythical tribe of warrior women who chose to live with one breast, the intention of the association is to use artistic creations to shine a positive light on the perception of life after mastectomy. The group is not anti-reconstruction but rather is working to make living with missing breasts as fashionable and socially acceptable as reconstruction.

Our first effort was an art exhibition in Luxembourg in 2008 which subsequently opened in central Paris. The show consisted of photography, paintings and sculpture. For the first time in France beautifully photographed Amazons, along with paintings and sculptures of asymmetric women, were on display. *Transcendence* (page 15) was chosen for the large promotional poster of the Paris exhibition and was displayed all over the capital city. Thousands of Parisians thus discovered asymmetric women, but again the media essentially ignored the event. In France it is common to see bare-breasted women in magazines and on beaches. But paradoxically the image of a single-breasted woman is still taboo—as indeed it is in most European countries.

Les amazones s'exposent was also active in encouraging Art Myers to continue photographing women after breast cancer and helped to facilitate the photography of additional subjects, all French. Their portraits and personal vignettes appear in this book. Luce, Cati, Lyne, Benedicte and I posed, as we all want to share the same message as the Americans before us, that life goes on after breast cancer and for some it can be even more rewarding. This ordeal, in confronting us with our own mortality, deeply encourages us to enjoy life to the fullest—now, immediately, and not wait for tomorrow.

by Annick Parent
Co-Founder of *les amazones s'exposent*
Author of *Itinéraire d'une amazone*
Ellébore Éditions, 2006

6

Introduction

Lorsque j'ai appris que j'allais devoir perdre un sein, j'ai demandé à l'hôpital à quoi j'allais ressembler, que l'on me montre des photographies de femmes devenues asymétriques. Aucune parole, aucune image ne me fut donnée en retour.

En France, l'ablation du sein est *tabou*. Si la plupart des femmes qui y sont confrontées restent telles qu'elles sont devenues, les médias ne parlent que des autres, celles qui ont choisi de faire une chirurgie réparatrice.

La découverte des photographies d'Art Myers a été une vraie révolution pour moi. Il y avait donc un au-delà du cancer, un au-delà de l'ablation du sein. Je découvrais des femmes, certes différentes par leur asymétrie, mais des femmes auxquelles je pouvais m'identifier : Andrea, Dani, Susan....

Dès ce jour, tout a changé. J'ai pu m'imaginer avec un seul sein sans angoisse. J'ai tout de suite eu envie que d'autres femmes puissent, elles aussi, profiter du message de vie, de liberté, transmis par nos sœurs américaines.

Avec Lillian Stirling, nous avons créé l'association « les amazones s'exposent », destinée à faire changer le regard porté sur le cancer à travers des créations artistiques. Nous ne sommes pas « contre » la reconstruction, nous nous attachons à faire en sorte que vivre avec un seul sein – ou plus de seins du tout – devienne socialement tout aussi acceptable que la chirurgie réparatrice.

Notre première réalisation fut une exposition de peintures, de sculptures et de photographies qui eut lieu au Grand Duché du Luxembourg en 2008, puis à l'Hôtel de Ville à

Paris. Ce fût la première fois, en France, que des Amazones étaient mises en valeur par de beaux clichés. « Transcendence » (page 15) fut choisie pour faire l'affiche de l'exposition à Paris, on la vit partout dans la capitale pendant quatre semaines. Des milliers de Parisiens ont ainsi découvert « l'asymétrie », mais la presse, elle, n'a pas relayé cet événement.

S'il est courant, dans notre pays, de voir des femmes les seins nus dans les magazines ou à la plage, paradoxalement l'image d'une femme à un seul sein est *tabou* - comme, d'ailleurs, dans la majeure partie des pays européens.

« Les amazones s'exposent » a également encouragé Art Myers à continuer à photographier des femmes après un cancer du sein, ainsi qu'à trouver de nouveaux modèles, toutes françaises. Leurs portraits ainsi que leurs textes sont publiés dans ce livre.

Luce, Cati, Lyne, Bénédicte et moi-même avons choisi de poser car nous voulons toutes faire passer le même message que les Américaines avant nous : au-delà du cancer, la vie continue, meilleure qu'avant même pour certaines.

Cette épreuve, qui fait prendre conscience de sa propre finitude, incite vivement à jouir de la vie maintenant, tout de suite, et non demain.

par Annick Parent
Co-Fondateur *les amazones s'exposent*
Auteur de *Itinéraire d'une amazone*
Ellébore Éditions, 2006

Sisterhood

Stephanie

*T*he mammograms were negative and the doctors assured me there was nothing to worry about. However, the quarter-sized lump in my right breast turned out to be cancer.

My breast and right arm took quite a beating after the lymphectomy, lymphadenectomy, surgery, radiation, and radioactive implants.

Over time my breast has again become fairly symmetrical. Now the solid mass on the outer side of my breast and the occasional ache and swelling in my arm remind me how precious each day is.

༂ Stephanie

Dora & Cy

Mastectomy at age 35, married 60 years

*W*hile I was in the hospital shortly after surgery, Cy's aunt was sitting by my bedside. I remember her saying, "Whatever you do, Dora, never let anyone see your scar, and especially never let Cy see it." I was devastated, but Cy being a super husband frowned on that comment. He has shared my problem with me for the past 52 years. ❧ Dora

*I*n 1942, when the surgeon called me into his office after completing a mastectomy on Dora, he leveled with me about the prospects for recovery. Even Dora's mother called me aside once and said, "We must not let Dora know that she's going to die." Her concern was devastating to me. I knew, however, that if it were I who faced an unpromising future Dora would be supportive in every way possible. I promised Dora that the operation would absolutely make no difference to me and that we would raise our three children together. ❧ Cy

Transcendence

Your hand touched symbols that filled the
    air with sonorous sounds.
    Your hand touched fountains that drenched the
    desert with ample water.
Your hand touched petals that colored the
    world with rainbow gardens.
Your hand touched sunlight that brightened
    raven tunnels with golden skies.
Your hand touched evening vines that intoxicated
    sorrows in desperate towns.
Your hand touched faces that occupied
    souls with endless laughter.
Your hand touched mine and softened
    this heart once made of stone.

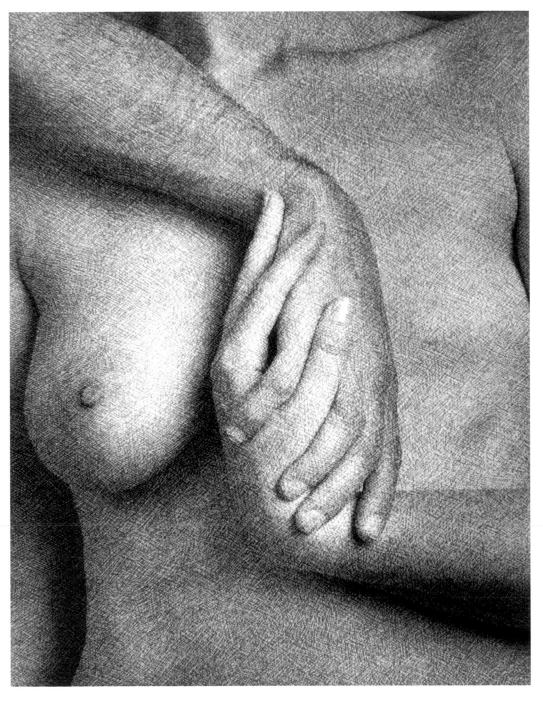

Joel and Doug
Reconstructed Right Breast

There is a bright side to everything! When I'm old and gravity has taken its toll, my implanted breast will remain erect like a sixteen-year-old's. ✎ Joel

When we are at a party and my wife says I can "nibble on her ear," I know it is time to leave-- you see, her earlobes were used to make nipples for her implanted breasts. ✎ Doug

17

Annick

*W*hen I learned during a routine mammography check-up that I had suspicious-looking micro-calcifications, I was afraid.

When the oncologist told me after the first operation that the results were bad, that I would have to have my whole breast removed, the world turned upside-down.

At that moment, I could never have imagined that I would get used to my androgynous bust and find a new freedom in this difference which is now me.

This adventure has freed me from the prescriptive attitudes which dictate the narrow margins of a suitable appearance for women, and above all, it has opened up a whole world of differences. ❧ Annick

Annick

Q uand j'ai appris, lors d'une mammographie de contrôl, que j'avais des micro-calcifications d'allure suspecte, j'ai eu peur.

Quand, après la première opération la cancérologue m'a dit que les résultats étaient mauvais, qu'il fallait m'enlever le sein en totalité, le monde a basculé.

Jamais je n'aurais imaginé, à ce moment-là, que j'apprivoiserai mon buste androgyne et trouverai une liberté nouvelle dans cette différence, qui maintenant me constitue.

Cette aventure m'a a affranchie des discours normatifs qui dictent aux femmes la marge étroite où se tenir, et surtout, elle m'a ouverte au monde de toutes les differences. ❧ Annick

Tanya

Left Mastectomy

*L*ive each day, each second, each morsel, to the fullest. Do what you want to do.

What a gift, at twenty-nine, to have had to face myself and ask: what do you regret, now that your life may be over? I live now in a manner that will allow me to answer that same question—forty-nine, sixty-nine, eighty-nine, whatever age— "NOTHING!"

I'll tell you the honest truth: I would not undo this gift of perspective, even to have my breast back.

I know, now, what is important, and what is not. ✍ Tanya

Hands That Still Nurture

I 've searched
    in many splendid seas
    and in many rapturous lands
but no one else has your rhythms,
    your shine,
    your earth.
Only you captivate the harmony from
    jaded birds.
Only you bring shade from green forests.
You are pure like a sleepless swan,
    true like an undulant river.
You give love like an endless horizon,
    you are the feathers that blanket my
    soul.
You are divine, golden, full.
And your emerald hands continue
    to nurture me.

Blair & Susan

*B*lair was in Naval flight training while I was going through chemo. Flight training is difficult enough, let alone being married—especially if your wife has cancer. On the day he was "winged," he gave me a dozen roses with a card that said, "You are the wind beneath my wings." Funny—I could have sworn it was the other way around.

                         ～ Susan

I used to look at Susan and see all the beauty, to long to be with her, to enjoy just touching her, to seek her comfort and warmth, to confide in my best friend, lover, and wife. Nothing has changed; I still do all of these. ～ Blair

Karen
Reconstructed Right Breast

*H*ow do I feel when a patient walks into the room for a mammogram? With some patients I am not aware of feeling anything. With others, those in particular who are feeling fear, I feel almost superior. After all, I have already been there. I have had breast cancer and I have had the radical treatment of a mastectomy. I now know what I will do in order to survive. I even have a new mound.

Then there are the patients with whom I choose to share my experience. Frankly, I am surprised at how many women want to see my reconstructed breast. ✎ Karen

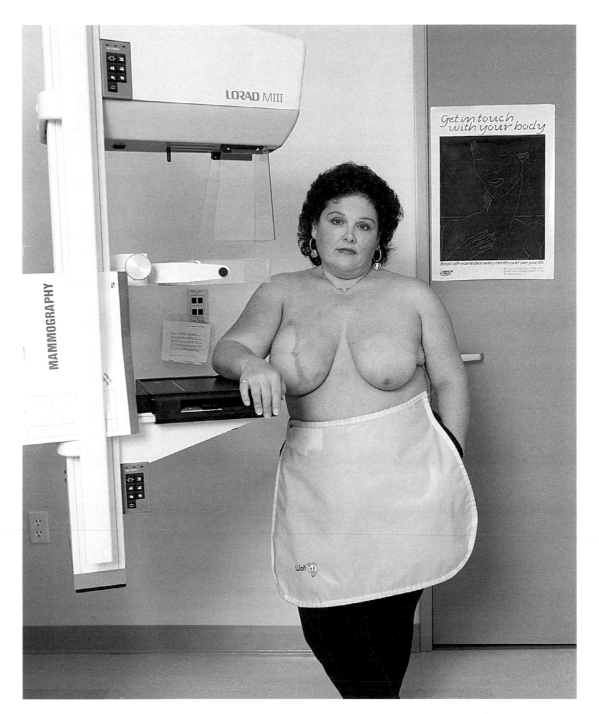

Venus & Friends

Venus smiles down
from the heavens.
Her cosmic wings
agape,
she stares at them.
Oh how beautiful!
She notices a woman
with missing parts.
She senses comfort,
a brilliant glaze.
Her soul moving, this woman,
guided by the spirit of
sun and wind.
She has something of her very
own.
It fills her up, it keeps her
company.

What a lovely woman,
who sends her freshness
out to sea,
who transcends humanity
with magical grace,
who naked is worth
a million statues.
A beauty sound like spring
full of incessant gifts.
An ambition higher than
an eager moon.
Venus ascends with calm
thought rich in her head.
She whispers,
that woman too is a
goddess.

Connie

When I was diagnosed I was devastated. A few years before, I was at my mother's side as she died of breast cancer. She fought her cancer in her own way, with a quiet dignity and unquestioning acceptance.

In my own struggle it was vital for me to become actively involved in my choices and treatment. After reading, talking to people in the cancer field and having several consultations with physicians, I found a team of doctors who viewed breast conservation as a viable treatment option.

The contrast between my experience and that of my mother's has led to some significant changes in my life: I became involved in patient support, returned to school and earned a PhD, and wrote my dissertation on "Choices and Options in Breast Cancer Decisions."

If I could give a gift to my sister, daughters and grand-daughters, it would be to see me as a living example of hope for the future. ❧ Connie

Cati

*L*osing one of my breasts suddenly didn't make me an Amazon in one day. The mastectomy was part of the protocol to fight against this cancer, so unbelievable for the age of 37.

Waking up and finding this vertiginous emptiness, this breast became a "phantom," invisible but always present in my brain. After finishing my chemo and x-rays, I thought about a surgical reconstruction. For my case, the only solution needed several operations and would hurt other parts of my body...hard decision to make. I even thought about an extreme solution: erase this wobbly part and remove the remaining breast...which of course and luckily no surgeon accepted to do.

I continued to have a love life, and was happily surprised: no man ran away, and one of them even succeeded to make this sole breast full of eroticism. The idea of a surgical reconstruction *was fading away, why suffer again? If it was not for the others, this reconstruction was then only for the image in the mirror…so I drowned this absent breast in a surplus of flesh (plus 15 kg). Then, bit by bit, the prosthesis became an accessory, just like make-up—good for appearance in society and removing it all when I please.*

I accepted this new body, practiced sports again, wore elegant clothes and then, one day, about six years after the removal, I evaluated and therefore concluded the obvious: I am an Amazon. The verb "to be," simply. The cancer took neither my life, nor my femininity.

Life decided that the second breast would develop a second cancer, operated exactly nine years after the first one, a "simple" tumorectomy but again chemo and x-rays. These pictures are the witness of this doubling, a momentarily bald Amazon. I hope that the intensity of continuing to live a sweet life is discernible at this very instant. ✎ Cati

Cati

Si j'ai perdu un sein de façon brutale, je ne suis pas devenue amazone en un jour. La mastectomie a été une partie du protocole de lutt cee contre cancer si surprenant pour mes 37 ans!

La découverte au réveil d'un vide vertigineux, puis ce sein est deveneu « fantôme », invisible mais toujours présent dans mon cerveau. Sortie des chimios et rayons, j'ai envisage une reconstruction chirurgicale. Pour mon cas, la seule solution possible nécessitait plusieurs interventions et constituait une atteinte à d'autres parties de mon corps (ventre, grande lèvre)… lourde décision à prendre. J'ai même envisage une solution radical: faire table rase de cette partie bancale et supprimer le sein restant…ce que bien sûr et heureusement aucun chirurgien n'a voulu entrendre.

J'ai continué à avoir une vie amoureuse, agréeable surprise: aucun homme n'est parti en courant, et l'un d'entre eux a su « recharger » ce seul sein de tout son érotisme. Le choix d'une *reconstruction chirurgicale s'éloignait doucement, pourquoi resouffrir? Si ce n'était pas pour les autres, cette reconstruction n'était donc plus destinée qu'à l'image du miroir...alors j'ai noyé ce sein absent dans un surplus de chairs (plus 15 kg). Puis doucement la prothèse est devenu un accessoire, au même titre que le maquillage: bien paraître en société et tout enlever quand ça me chante.*

J'ai accepté ce nouveau corps, j'ai refait du sport, remis des tenues élégantes...et un jour, environ six ans après l'ablation, j'ai formulé, donc intégré cette evidence: Je suis une amazone. Du verbe « être » simplement. Le cancer ne m'a pris ni ma vie ni ma féminité!

La vie a voulu que le second sein développe un second cancer, opéré exactement neuf ans après le premier, tumorectomie « simple » mais rechimio et rayons. Le photo d'Art est le témoin de ce double, amazone momentanément chauve. J'espère que la rage de continuer une vie douce se perçoit au coeur de cet instant. ❧ Cati

Andrea & Richard
Double Mastectomy

*A*ndrea was deeply concerned and, at times, depressed about her appearance after the first mastectomy. Aside from empathizing, I can honestly say that I never gave that a second thought. Her breasts never had a great deal to do with my intense attraction for her. Andrea's sexiness emanates from something inherent and essential in her persona. If anything, that energy has been intensified by her struggle to survive.

           ❧ Richard

*I*t was very funny. I went to the water slides with my eleven-year-old daughter and her best friend, Max. We went down the waterfall, which pushes you up and forward. When I climbed out of the pool, I found that one of my velcroed prostheses was gone! I went over to the young lady in charge and said, "We have a problem—one of my prostheses is in the pool." She looked at me with a question on her face—she had no idea what a prosthesis was. At that moment, Max shouted, "There it is," and sure enough, it was floating toward us on the current. He jumped in and retrieved it for me. Next time I went down the waterfall I held my "boobs."

           ❧ Andrea

My Hands, My Body

It is her body, her hands
however unshaped and plain,
they are her own.
A body like a sublime cloud that drifts into the cool skies.
Hands like two peculiar plums saturated with sweet dew.
Can she caress?
Yes.
Her fingers make blossoms of everything.
Can her body speak?
Indeed.
Her sculpture lines rave poetic tones.
Can she love?
Completely,
her whole being is a treasure full of
spectacular gems giving the world
immense, peaceful light.

Yavonne
Reconstructed Left Breast

After finishing treatment, I could only think about getting back to my old self again. Being twenty-eight and single I wasn't comfortable with having to stuff one side of my bra and hope it wouldn't move in the course of the day. So having the reconstruction was the ideal thing for me.

My breast wasn't what I missed the most; it was my hair. It was pretty hilarious when it happened. It came out in clumps. I couldn't stand the anticipation of the rest coming out on its own so I called my sister and she came over and looked at me kind of solemn and we both busted up laughing. Then she shaved the remainder off. My two daughters also laughed at this hysterical event.

The funniest thing that happened to me was when my boyfriend spent the night. At that time I was wearing a wig. He'd never seen my head before. One night in bed I had one too many of my hot flashes, as my hormones were all screwed up. I took the wig off while he was asleep and it put it on my pillow. I figured if he awoke I'd put it back on. But I fell asleep and must have looked like a lollipop laying on a pillow. He woke up before me and he tried to play it off but I know it was shocking to him. We laughed about it later. ❧ Yavonne

44

Yavonne Reclining

An important part of going through my breast cancer experience was the fact that it did not make me feel unattractive or take away the sensual feelings about myself.

          Ȣ Yavonne

Dani & Ralph

One day, long before I met my sweetheart Ralph, I stood naked in front of the mirror and made peace with the smooth mastectomy scar where my breast once was. I decided to truly feel beautiful. Later, after a romantic weekend in Mexico, Ralph called to tell me: "I love the asymmetry of your chest." I smiled and laughed to myself—thinking of how hard he must have thought to come up with the perfect compliment. ❧ Dani

I didn't meet Dani until long after her illness, surgery and treatment. What became immediately obvious to me about her was a bright, shining spirit like no one else's. An even greater surprise to me was to learn that this spirit and outlook are infectious. I've caught them too. ❧ Ralph

Benedicte

*T*ime...

To accept, to take the time necessary to recognize, to familiarize, to love
    this different body.
And finally, once past the moment of despair, fear, revolt and anger, to get
    slowly in touch again with the "essence" of your femininity, your
    femininity present as always and maybe even more.
To look at yourself simply and to be looked at serenely like here,
    without wanting to drop the gaze or to look the other way: To Be.
To savor, to taste the happiness of living the "essential" of every instant.

I would like this picture to be a message of life, hope and
encouragement for all women facing this destabilizing
experience. Six years ago, after the announcement of the
diagnosis, I was completely panicked: How will I go out into
the street? How will I ever dare to be naked in front of a man
again, to be loved? How could I live without a reconstruction?

And life goes on....
And now, always a woman: first a woman with maybe the addition of
    one less breast.
And time becomes more precious...each second is a rich treasure.

                                         ❧ Benedicte

Bénédicte

*L*e temps...

Accepter, prendre le temps nécessaire pour reconnaître, apprivoiser, aimer ce corps différent.

Et enfin, passé le moment du désespoir, de la peur, de la révolte, de la colère, se laisser doucement recontacter « l'essence » même de sa féminité toujours aussi présente et peut-être même plus encore.

Se regarder simplement et se laisser regarder sereinement comme ici, sans le désir de baisser ni détourner le regard : « Être »

Savourer, déguster le bonheur de vivre « L'essentiel » de chaque instant .

J'aimerais que cette photo soit un message de vie, d'espoir et de réconfort pour toutes les femmes confrontées à cette épreuve déstabilisante. Il y a 6 ans à l'annonce du diagnostic, c'était la panique la plus totale : Comment vais-je sortir dans la rue ? Comment oserais-je me montrer nue à un homme, me laisser aimer ? Comment peut-on vivre sans reconstruction ?

Et le cheminement se fait….

Et maintenant, toujours femme, femme d'abord avec peut-être en plus un sein en moins.

Et le temps, devient plus précieux … chaque seconde est un trésor de richesse. ✌ Bénédicte

Susan Reclining in Striated Light

I sat on the edge of the bed, facing away from him. "Ready?" I asked. "I'm ready," he replied, the unwavering tone of his voice giving me a sense of surety. I turned my body to face him. He studied my single breast, then the inverted contour and long scar (I call it my "badge of courage") on the other side with attentiveness and gentleness. Turning his warm gaze toward my eyes, he whispered, "You're beautiful," as he embraced me with all the tenderness and passion that has become us.

It was that easy. I wasn't always sure it would be after my divorce. My (ex) husband had been so understanding and wonderful. But when he left, I had to grapple with the questions that all "single boobed, single babes" face. Will anyone find me attractive? Will anyone be able to look past the cancer and the scars and see the real me?

Of course I had never lost sight of my beauty. To me, having lost a breast never equated with the loss of my femininity, my sensuality, my strength. It was all there. It is all there. Funny thing is, my personal body image is much better now than it was before. In the past it was always, "I need to lose a few pounds," or "My boobs are uneven." Now I look in the mirror and think, "You look damn good." Even the times—and there are many—when I "forget" and surprise myself looking in the mirror, I have to smile.

We smile a lot, Rob and I. We'll be married April twentieth.

⮞ Susan

Sometimes a Leaf Will Fall Before Autumn

Sometimes an easy comfort
    comes from a stranger's bliss.
Sometimes we know more
    than the highest mountains.
Sometimes courage is just the price of living.
Sometimes our biggest obstacles
    lead to naked paths.
Sometimes the loneliest times
    are when we are surrounded.
Sometimes warm hands
    can quiet angry sirens.
Sometimes being free
    means losing your carefulness.
Sometimes true beauty
    can never be captured.
Sometimes heartache
    is the only way to understand love.
Sometimes our greatest strength
    is in being vulnerable.
And,
Sometimes a leaf will fall before autumn.

Carol

My first mission was to cut off my waist-long hair and have it made into a wig. I couldn't bear the thought of wearing something that wasn't me. For the longest time, though, I did without it, wearing scarves and hats, and cultivating an exotic look. But soon I was too cold and had to wear the wig. Finally, when I had not a single hair on my head, there was no way to keep the wig on. So I wore colorful, tail-streaming headbands—Indian-style. My first little victory. My hair grew back with a vengeance, thicker and wavier than ever. I still wear headbands from time to time, a reminder and a smile.

I returned to my daily swimming at the gym. Timidly. At first, I went over late at night, when I knew the locker room would be empty. I undressed and dressed under a sweatshirt, maneuvering my clothes like Houdini. Each night I became more daring and went earlier and earlier. Finally I was changing and swimming as I always had. Another little victory. But I couldn't help wondering: if the incidence of breast cancer was one in nine, where, in my fifteen years of swimming, were all the women with mastectomies? Why had I never seen one in the locker room? My fear was born of theirs, as was my sense of disfigurement and embarrassment. But now I had chosen otherwise, and so my victory came, gradually and nourishingly. ❧ Carol

Luce

With one less breast
My body becomes unique
So, love it!
A touch of singularity
A true lesson of humility?
Never forget:
Envelope of the body, always legitimate.

Different!
I have always felt different!
One less breast?
One more unique trait!
And the feeling of belonging
In a large and new family:
Those of the Amazons!
Beautiful name, wouldn't you say?
But even more
And that's the essential:
Belonging to the LIVING!

❧ Luce

Luce

Avec un sein en moins
Mon corps devient unique
Alors, pour cela, aimez-le !
Zeste de singularité
Ou vraie leçon d'humilité ?
Ne jamais oublier :
Enveloppe du corps, toujours, vaut légitimité.

Différente !
Je me suis toujours sentie différente !
Un sein en moins ?
Une singularité en plus !
Et le sentiment d'appartenir
A une grande et nouvelle famille :
Celle des amazones !
Joli nom n'est-ce pas ?
Mais plus encore
Et c'est là l'essentiel :
A celle des VIVANTS !

∽ Luce

Lisa & Scotty

Scotty's sportster is fast. The lines to the bike are straight and hard, which lends itself to being ridden in the same manner. It suits him because he likes to ride on the edge, push his limitations.

Me, I like to cruise and take in the scenery. The shape and lines to my bike are much different than Scotty's, full and round. Scotty says my FLH rides like a Cadillac. Both bikes are powerful and responsive, but there's a definite difference in style and feel to each bike. I think we both enjoy the same aspects of the bikes but for different reasons.

ॐ Lisa

Lisa With Barbell

I've made changes, reshaped my body with the use of free weights and aerobics over the last twelve years. And the surgeon made his changes when he removed my breast. A bit odd perhaps, but I enjoy the change in that when I look at my chest where he removed my breast, I can truly appreciate and enjoy the shape and lines that I have added to my body over the years with the weights. The contrast is appealing to me, a soft breast on one side and a hard "pec" on the other. ❧ Lisa

To Touch, Perchance to Feel

See this radiant body,
how I bask in its sensual delight.
Smooth and blush,
with bareness made to tempt.
I stroke this honeysuckle leanness,
and caress at lithe flesh,
only to relish in the pleasure of being a woman.
I feel the warmth. I smell the skin.
It smells like a baby, fresh and innocent.
I touch the softness that changed my destiny,
and think how marvelous to feel, to exist.
My hands break deep into me
reaching my soul.
Reaching this brilliant being.
And all splendid eyelids
are on this perfect woman.

Ulla
Partial Mastectomy

If you look at my photograph I want you to see that breast cancer need not disfigure you or end your life—only as much as you allow it to happen. Cancer is a rough disease to handle! However, you have the choice to enjoy every moment of your life now or let cancer take over.

ҩ Ulla

Carol and Dick

Dick, the love for the rest of my life, is my soul-mate. He feels my pain retroactively and yearns to have eased it. But the legacy of that pain is what we share: a zest for life, a compelling belief in the here-and-now, and a knowledge of victory and grace. He has made song of the more the more. ❧ Carol

My mother died of breast cancer and I have always felt that I didn't do enough for her in her waning years. Little did I realize, when I met this lean, flat-chested beauty, that she would be my salvation. Not only has she given me a love that I never thought was possible, but every time I return that love, I feel my mother's spirit shining down on both of us.

❧ Dick

Lyne & Jean Philippe

*I*n my bed at the hospital following my surgery, a mastectomy, I asked the nurse, "Tell me, my breast, where have you put it? Where is it now?"

I asked because I would have liked to say "bye" to this unhealthy breast, fortunately removed. ❧ Lyne

Lyne et Famille

Après ma mastectomie, dans mon lit d'hôpital, j'ai demandé à l'infirmière, « Il est où, maintenant, mon sein? »

J'avais juste besoin de dire encore une fois « au revoi r» à ce sein malsain qu'on m'avait heureusement enlevé. ❧ Lyne

Painted Ladies

As an avid bodysurfer, I have discovered that wearing a bathing suit top, while required by law, is an incredible nuisance. With only one breast to hold it up, the bathing suit acts as a giant scoop for sand and seaweed. Frustrated, I inquired of an attorney friend what she thought a judge would say if I were to go topless and be hauled into court. She told me that the "standard of proof" is fifty percent plus one, and that I would be always one percent shy of a conviction. She did however, advise me to be as discreet as possible to avoid the fuss of handcuffs and the like.

Topless bodysurfing became part of my routine. One day, while preparing for the World Bodysurfing Championships with a girlfriend, I placed my swimming fins in front of my chest and nonchalantly slipped my top off, keeping my fins up front for cover. As I walked out into the surf, my friend laughed as she dramatically closed one eye and said, "Let's go!"

Art and I decided that we needed a humorous photo in this project to reflect a shared spirit of acceptance. One magical afternoon the three of us served as canvases for the artist, Pam Stuart. Accompanied by a chorus of laughter and giggles, I became "the wink." Carol was transformed into a woman with cleavage in a beautiful blue camisole. This was a special gift to her husband who had met her years after her double mastectomy. Susan, with theatrical flair, became comedy and tragedy, with each intentionally reversed so that the comedy mask appeared over the mastectomy scar.

This trio of "Painted Ladies" shares a poignant bond. From Carol to Dani to Susan, we each served as mentor and friend to each other when we were diagnosed. Years later we celebrated our friendships in living color. ❧ Dani

Paris Exhibition

Hotel de Ville

About the Photographer

    As well as being a fine art photographer, Art Myers is a physician specializing in preventive medicine and public health. He graduated from the Philadelphia College of Osteopathic Medicine and received his post-doctoral degree in public health from the Graduate School of Public Health, San Diego State University. Although largely self-taught in photography he has studied in workshops with Annie Leibovitz, Arnold Newman, Larry Fink, Sally Mann, Joyce Tenneson and other well-known artists. His photographs have been exhibited in numerous galleries and museums in the United States and Europe.

    Maria Marrocchino works in advertising in New York City. She has been writing poetry since she was a child. This is the first time that her poems have appeared in a book.